Strange
School
Stories

Look for other

titles:

Strange School Stories

by Mary Packard

and the Editors of Ripley Entertainment Inc.

illustrations by Ron Zalme

SCHOLASTIC INC.

New York   Toronto   London   Auckland   Sydney
Mexico City   New Delhi   Hong Kong   Buenos Aires

Developed by Nancy Hall, Inc.
Designed by R studio T
Cover design by Atif Toor
Photo research by Laura Miller

ISBN 0-439-68774-8

12 11 10 9 8 7 6 5 4 3 2   4 5 6 7 8 9/0

Printed in the U.S.A.

First printing, October 2004

Contents

Strange School Stories

Introduction

The Best Odd-ucation

Welcome to the weird and wonderful world of Ripley's Believe It or Not!, where no fact is too bizarre, no deed is too extreme, and no person is too strange. For Robert Ripley, creator of Believe It or Not!, ordinary meant dull, and the word *normal* was not in his vocabulary. Everything about Ripley was over the top, from his bright pink

shirts to his polka-dot bow ties. So as we delve into the very serious subject of education, we'll shine a spotlight on the unconventional side of the school experience—those aspects that are not defined by order and rules, but by disorder, chance, and whimsy.

Robert Ripley believed that rules should never be carved in stone, and he was able to convert many others to his way of thinking. Just an average student, Ripley was a naturally gifted salesman, allowing him to talk his teachers into letting him hand in illustrations instead of the essays his classmates were required to write.

In this book you will read about other average students who made good, such as talk-show host David Letterman. You will also learn about such things as the value of class clowns, how juggling can improve grades,

ELF CHART

and the link between hair type and intelligence. And where else could you find out about Russian students who had to pay for the privilege of taking a bathroom break or the professor who is an expert on elf history? These are the kinds of facts that Robert Ripley always had on the tip of his tongue to amuse his friends.

For Ripley, dates and formulas had their place, but so did daydreams and flights of fancy. As you will see, some of the world's most gifted geniuses were daydreamers who

barely made passing grades when they were in school. Even the great Albert Einstein was considered slow in school, and Thomas Edison's father feared that his son would never amount to anything!

So get ready to read the weirdest, funniest, most bizarre facts about school that have ever been assembled in one place. Test your I.Q. with the Whiz Quizzes and Brain Busters in each chapter, then try the pop quiz and use the Ripley's scorecard to see how well you did. Remember, coloring outside of the lines is cool. There will be no raising of hands, mistakes will be encouraged, and daydreaming is expected of all.

Believe It!®

CHAPTER 1

Odd-inary Students

From attending classes six days a week to literally lying down on the job, there are as many ways to be a student as there are subjects to study.

Whiz Quiz!

Students attend school six days a week, including Saturdays, in . . .

a. Puerto Rico.
b. Sweden.
c. Japan.
d. Spain.

It's Greek to Me!

If more students knew the derivation of the word *school*, they might use it as an excuse to goof off. *School* is derived from the Greek word *schole*, which means "leisure"!

Letter Perfect: Many C students have talents that won't earn them a place on the honor roll, but that doesn't mean they don't deserve a shot at success. Talk-show host David Letterman, who admits to having been a C student himself, dedicated a classroom in the School of Broadcasting at his alma mater, Indiana's Ball State University, "to all C students before me and after me." He also set up the David Letterman Scholarship, which awards as much as $10,000 for an outstanding creative project. No minimum grade point average is required to be eligible.

Serious Business: In Almelo, the Netherlands, playing hooky can be a criminal offense. Children as young as 12 years old who have a habit of cutting school could end up going to jail. The policy, first put into effect in January 2004, is aimed at repeat offenders between the ages of 12 and 16.

Stifle Yourself! Have you noticed that yawning can be contagious? Within five minutes of seeing someone else yawn, 55 percent of people end up yawning themselves. Now you know why it's not uncommon to see an entire class of students yawning at the same time.

Whiz Quiz!

Nine United States presidents: George Washington, Andrew Jackson, Martin Van Buren, Zachary Taylor, Millard Fillmore, Abraham Lincoln, Andrew Johnson, Grover Cleveland, and Harry Truman . . .

a. graduated from college at the top of their class.
b. flunked out of college.
c. did not attend college.
d. were expelled from college for playing practical jokes.

Pet-degree: The National Audubon Society Expedition Institute in Belfast, Maine, awarded a college degree in environmental studies to a dog. Timber, a Norwegian elkhound, earned the honorary degree by traveling 200,000 miles with students from the institute.

School Craze:

In 1939, a classmate bet Harvard University freshman Lothrop Withington $10 that he wouldn't swallow a live goldfish. Withington took the bet and, since he was running for class president, invited his classmates to attend the event. On March 3, a crowd watched as Withington dropped a wriggling goldfish into his mouth and swallowed it. Withington won the bet, lost the election, and made the Boston newspapers. Soon goldfish-swallowing was a hot new fad, with college students around the country vying to see who could swallow the most live fish.

Bad Timing:

Stuart Carter, a graduating senior at Roseburg High School in Oregon, was scheduled to receive a special award for perfect attendance—but he was absent on the day the honors were awarded!

Whiz Quiz!

In 1982, freshman Scott Ritter defeated 4,513 contestants in a two-hour-long musical chairs contest at Ohio State University. His prize was . . .

a. one free pizza a week for a year.
b. a leather reclining chair.
c. free concert tickets for the rest of the school year.
d. $4,513.

Double Take:

Meet Lorraine and Loretta Syzmanski of Pittsburgh, Pennsylvania—and Lorraine and Loretta Syzmanski of Pittsburgh, Pennsylvania. Both sets of twins attended the same school, were in the same class, and lived in the same neighborhood, but were not related in any way!

Something's Fishy: In 2002, while on a field trip with her class, a young girl got robbed by a most unusual culprit—a trout swimming in the Aquarium of the Lakes in Windermere, England. Perhaps the frisky fish mistook the money for food when it jumped out of the water and yanked the cash (£5, or about $9) right out of the girl's hand. The astonished curator said that it was the only time he'd ever seen a student robbed by a trout.

That's Using Their Heads:

An advertising agency in England called Cunning Stunts has invented a new way to advertise their clients' products—using students' foreheads as billboards. The agency offers students the equivalent of about $140 per week to wear a transfer made of nontoxic vegetable dye that displays a corporate logo on their forehead for a minimum of three hours a day.

Short Division:

To save money on school expenses, the parents of four-year-old identical twin boys sent their sons to preschool in Chongqing, China, on alternate days of the week. For six months in 2003, one of the boys attended the school on even days, and the other boy on odd days, until the teachers finally figured out what was going on!

Holding Pattern:

For a brief period in 2003, students in need of a bathroom break at a high school in the Russian city of Taganrog first had to be sure that they had enough cash. It all started after some students vandalized a bathroom. To raise money for repairs, school officials decided to make students pay for the privilege of using the toilet. Kids short of money would just have to hold it. After city authorities got wind of the scheme, the bathroom tax was dropped. Students at the school were very relieved.

No Average Joe:

In 1957, Joe College was a student at St. Joseph's College in Philadelphia, Pennsylvania.

Whiz Quiz!

On their way to school, girls in Guinea, Africa . . .

a. balance their schoolbooks on their heads.
b. let monkeys carry their books.
c. ride on elephants.
d. ride in canoes.

Lying Down on the Job: A study done at Colgate University in New York found that students were better at solving math problems when lying down with their feet propped up. While reclining, the students solved problems 7.4 percent faster and got 14 percent more of them right than they did while sitting at their desks.

School in a Box: Every year, schools all over the world are destroyed by floods, earthquakes, and war. Now, displaced students can continue their studies, thanks to Unicef's School-in-a-Box kits. Of course you can't fit an entire school in a box, but you can fill it with enough pencils, paper, crayons, teaching materials, and workbooks for 40 kids.

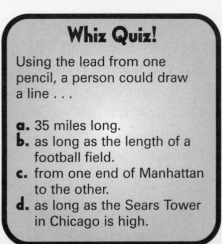

Whiz Quiz!

Using the lead from one pencil, a person could draw a line . . .

a. 35 miles long.
b. as long as the length of a football field.
c. from one end of Manhattan to the other.
d. as long as the Sears Tower in Chicago is high.

Clowning Around:

Let's hear it for classroom clowns! It seems that kids learn more easily in classes that have a class clown than in classes that don't. According to Professor Sandra Domico of the University of Florida, humor acts as a tension breaker, creating a relaxed environment for learning to take place.

Sleeping on It:

Researchers have found that the best time to study is right before bed. That's because students remember new facts learned during that time period better than any other. The closer to bedtime students study, the more information they will remember.

Prime Mischief Maker:

In December 2003, Dutch Prime Minister Jan Peter Balkenende visited an elementary school in Overechtl, Holland. In one class, the teacher and students had their picture taken with their honored guest. Imagine their embarrassment when they saw that one of the students had put up two fingers behind the prime minister's head as a joke. All was forgiven after the mischief maker wrote a letter to Balkenende apologizing for the prank.

Lousy Trick:

Some students will try anything to get out of going to class. In 1981, a few students in Stuttgart, Germany, paid the equivalent of $2.60 each for lice to put into their hair. The kids were excused from school, but when their parents found out what they'd done, the kids had to pay more than money for their trick!

Never Give Up:

Robert F. Kennedy (1925–1968) was the United States Attorney General from 1961 to 1964, and a New York State senator from 1964 to 1968—accomplishments no one would have expected of him the year he flunked third grade!

Watt's Up? Thomas Edison (1847–1931), inventor of the lightbulb and holder of more than 1,090 patents when he died, was mostly self-educated. Edison's first teacher told the seven-year-old boy's mother that he was "addled" (confused) and asked too many questions. Within three months, his mother had taken Edison out of school. From then on, most of his education took place at home.

Whiz Quiz!

For good behavior, students in Chinese elementary schools receive . . .

a. silver medals.
b. blue ribbons.
c. purple patches for their blazers.
d. red handkerchiefs.

Fruity Idea:
Florida's state fruit is the orange, and Georgia's is the peach, so when fourth graders at Veterans Memorial Elementary School in Brick, New Jersey, found out

that their state had no official fruit, they went to work. The students chose the blueberry, a fruit that was first cultivated in New Jersey. Then they lobbied the state congress for legislation to make their choice official. Their efforts paid off in January 2004, when Governor James McGreevey took up their cause and declared the blueberry the official state fruit of New Jersey.

Everything Is Relative: World-class mathematical genius Albert Einstein (1879–1955), author of the general theory of relativity, was considered very slow by his parents and teachers. He did not even learn to speak until he was six years old! Perhaps, instead of talking, young Albert was thinking deep thoughts.

Fieldwork: In 2004, students in Swaziland began their school year a week late. Why? King Mswati III postponed the first day of school so that boys could take part in weeding the royal fields—one of the most sacred rituals in the country. Many parents were critical of this new decree, which affected 30,000 public school students. No word on how the students felt about it.

On the Straight and Narrow: Jay R. Sand of Jersey City, New Jersey, started his education at Harry Moore Public School, went on to attend Snyder High School, and then St. Peter's College—all of which were located on the same street.

Whiz Quiz!

The word for "fear of going to school" is . . .

a. tskaidekaphobia.
b. miserecolephobia.
c. neinschuleophobia.
d. didaskaleinophobia.

It's Never Too Late: Even though Kimani Murage of Kenya is 84 years old, he has recently begun attending school, where most of his classmates are just seven. In fact, two of his grandchildren are in higher grades than he is. Murage decided to start school after primary education became free in Kenya in 2003. He hopes to fulfill his childhood dream of becoming a veterinarian. Way to go, Kimani!

Ahead of His Time: In 1982, Jay Luo, the son of Taiwanese immigrants, became the youngest student in United States history to graduate from college. He received a math degree from Idaho's Boise State University at the age of twelve.

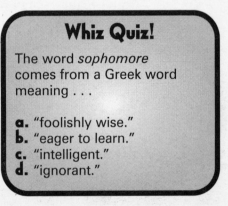

Whiz Quiz!

The word *sophomore* comes from a Greek word meaning . . .

a. "foolishly wise."
b. "eager to learn."
c. "intelligent."
d. "ignorant."

Turning Over a New Leash:  Children who have always longed for a puppy now have a new reason to persuade their parents to give in. According to a recent study conducted by psychologist Reinhold Bergler at the University of Bonn in Germany, children who have dogs are better behaved, more motivated, and get better grades than children who don't!

Going Places: Before he was two years old, Greg Smith could name all the dinosaurs that ever lived. At the age of nine, he graduated from high school with honors, and in May 2003, at 13, he graduated from Randolph-Macon College in Virginia. That's not all. In July 2001, Greg  founded International Youth Advocates, an organization that lobbies on behalf of underprivileged children. No doubt that's also why, at the age of 13, Greg Smith was the youngest person ever to be nominated for the Nobel Peace Prize!

Getting There: If you don't live close enough to walk, a bus is one way to get to school. So is a boat, like the ones some children in Brazil take. Lots of kids in Scandinavian countries get to school on skis, while Nanay students in Siberia arrive on skis pulled by dogs. Children in Alaska ride on snowmobiles to get to school. Probably the most adventurous way of all to travel is the method used by many South American children living in the rain forest. They zip above the treetops on a cable that stretches from one end of a valley to the other! Believe It or Not!

Whiz Quiz!

To protect the students from the hot sun, hats are part of the school uniform in . . .

a. Kenya.
b. Bermuda.
c. Jamaica.
d. Australia.

Brain Buster

It's time for a test! Get ready to find out how good you are at telling which facts are truly loony and which are downright false!

Robert Ripley dedicated his life to seeking out the bizarre and unusual. But every unbelievable thing he recorded was proven to be true. In the Brain Buster at the end of every chapter, you'll play Ripley's role—trying to verify the fantastic facts presented. Each Ripley's Brain Buster contains a group of four shocking statements. But of these so-called "facts," **one** is **fiction**. Will you **Believe It!** or **Not!**?

Wait—there's more! Following the Brain Busters are special bonus games or questions where you can earn extra points! Keep score by flipping to the end of the book for the answer key and a scorecard.

Check it out! School is for learning lessons—and one important lesson to learn is to not believe everything you read. Can you tell which of the facts below you can believe and which one is not only unbelievable but untrue?

a. In Germany, children receive a large paper cone filled with school supplies, presents, and candy on their first day in kindergarten.

Believe It!   **Not!**

21

b. In China, children get to take their pet pandas to school once a month.

Believe It!   **Not!**

c. In Japan, children take two pairs of shoes to school, one pair to wear inside and one pair to wear at recess.

Believe It!   **Not!**

d. On the first day of school in Kazakhstan, one child is chosen to be carried around the room and introduced to the other students.

Believe It!   **Not!**

• •

BONUS GAME
Have a Nice Trip!

Match the city to a place where students who live there might go on a field trip.

1. Beijing, China

2. Tokyo, Japan

3. New York City, USA

4. Paris, France

5. Cuzco, Peru

6. Cairo, Egypt

a. The Metropolitan Museum of Art

b. Machu Picchu

c. The Eiffel Tower

d. The Great Wall

e. The Sphinx

f. Ueno Zoo

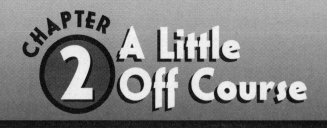

Most schools offer English, math, and science, but to find out where you can take an oddball course or to bone up on the latest wacky research, you need look no further!

Whiz Quiz!

In a study at Bowling Green State University in Ohio, psychobiology researcher Jaak Panksepp discovered that . . .

a. chimpanzees can make and use tools.
b. pigs can be trained to play computer games.
c. rats make happy chirping noises when tickled.
d. mice that eat nothing but rice get depressed.

TV 101: In the 1980s, Boston University got a grant from the United States Office of Education to teach college students the correct way to watch television. *Duh!*

Rock On: Recent cutbacks in music programs have left a lot of gifted students with no way to develop their talent. Now, a program called Little Kids Rock, started by David Wish in 2001, provides instruments and trains teachers to help kids learn about rock, hip-hop, blues, and other musical styles they're interested in. Famous musicians sometimes visit classes to give budding musicians tips on how to make it in the business.

Roadkill 101: At Hayden Valley Elementary School in Colorado, second and fourth graders are taking a course called "Critter Control" to learn how to track dead animals on the highway. Using the software program GIS (Geographic Information System), students map out the areas on U.S. Highway 40 that are the most dangerous to wildlife. In five years, the students hope to have enough data to suggest where to place new animal-crossing signs, reduced-speed areas, and animal-sized culverts.

Math-letes: At the Gateway School in St. Louis, Missouri, math and science are so much fun that you find kids doing school projects on the unusual playground designed by landscape architect Herb Schaal. A walkway filled with brightly colored cones is actually a mini geometry lesson. Kids can take the cones apart to uncover a circle, an

ellipse, and other geometric shapes. A solar system built to scale allows students to experience firsthand the relative position of the planets and their size in relation to one another. Kids can even study nature in a wetlands area protected by a boardwalk.

Whiz Quiz!

In 1978, students at Indiana University could receive credit for taking a course called . . .

a. "How to Play Checkers."
b. "Comic Book Studies."
c. "Monopoly for Fun and Profit."
d. "Muppet Mania."

Juggling Classes: Anyone who's ever tried juggling knows that it's harder than it looks. However, David Finnigan, creator of the Juggling for Success school program, guarantees that if you practice, you'll not only learn to juggle but also gain self-confidence and improve your academic performance in such subjects as reading, writing, and math. Teachers in the more than 400 elementary schools that use his classroom-based program agree.

Shipping News:
For those of you interested in cruising the seven seas, the University of Plymouth in England offers a degree in cruise operations management.

Whiz Quiz!

Researchers at England's University of Leicester conducted a study to find out if playing certain kinds of music would . . .

a. keep mosquitoes from biting.
b. encourage zoo animals to mate.
c. cause grass to grow faster.
d. encourage cows to produce more milk.

Calling All Slackers: Why major in physics or English literature when at many colleges you can get a degree in leisure studies and recreation? Some of the required courses include "Foundations of Leisure," "Principles of Recreation," "Theory of Pool/Spa Operation," and "Play in America." You can even continue your studies after graduation and get a master's degree or Ph.D. in the same field.

Some Nerve! Research completed by Dr. Peter R. Huttenlocher, Professor of Pediatrics and Neurology at the University of Chicago, Illinois, showed that the number of nerve connections in the frontal cortex—the part of the brain involved in reasoning—is highest between the ages of two and eight. By the time a person reaches adulthood, the number of connections has declined by about 50 percent. Perhaps this is the reason young children learn more quickly than adults.

Tongue-in-Cheek: Scientists at Swansea University in Wales have conducted a most unusual study with very strange results. It seems that 80 percent of the life-science students they studied could curl their tongues into vertical tubes. They concluded that the gene that controls tongue curling is linked to the one that causes a person to be interested in science!

Filling the Information Gap: When fifth graders at Endeavor Elementary School in Issaquah, Washington, discovered that there were only three pages in their entire American history book on slavery from the 1600s to the 1800s, they took matters into their own hands. Encouraged by their teacher, Eric Ensey, the students researched the subject to find out everything they could.

Then they created a web site called "Never Again: Students Explore the Slavery Experience," so they could share the results of their study with other students.

Grasping at Straws: In Berlin, Germany, a farmers' organization established the city's first straw kindergarten in an old factory building in 2004. More than 220 bales of straw were spread out over the floor for kids to play in.

Why? To give young city children the chance to experience a bit of farm life.

Awesome Akwesasne: Like many Native American languages, that of the Mohawks was disappearing— until recently. Now children at the Akwesasne Freedom School in Rooseveltown, New York, speak only Kanien'kehá:ka (gah-nyah-gay-HA-gah), the language of the Mohawk people. The students use their Mohawk names, sing Mohawk songs, and learn Mohawk dances.

Fourth-grader Kahéntawaks (gah-HON-dah-walks) proudly explains that her Mohawk name means "She Sways with the Grass." It's not hard to see why the Mohawks would want to keep their beautiful language alive.

Whiz Quiz!

In 2001, the University of Illinois in Urbana-Champaign offered a course called "History 298" that was all about . . .

a. singer Elvis Presley.
b. author Betty Friedan.
c. cartoonist Charles Schulz.
d. TV talk-show host Oprah Winfrey.

29

Prime Time: For two years, more than 60,000 computers all over the world were involved in the search for the largest prime number. It was Michael Shafer, a graduate student at Michigan State University, who finally came up with the answer. Unfortunately, we can't tell you what it is because printing the 6,320,430-digit number would take up 1,500 pages!

Poking Around: If you're an undergraduate at the School of Agricultural and Natural Resource Sciences at Sul Ross State University in Alpine, Texas, you can take courses on how to shoe a horse; judge livestock; manufacture sausage; and slaughter cattle, sheep, and hogs. You can also participate in college rodeo, which began at Sul Ross, and compete in bronco riding, roping and wrestling steers, and more. If you're really good, you might even win a scholarship for outstanding achievement in rodeo!

Special Interest Groups: These days there's a college scholarship for everyone. Too short for a basketball scholarship? Not to worry. The Billy Barty Foundation offers several scholarships for students less than 4 feet 10 inches tall. Perhaps you'd like to study Klingon for your foreign language requirement? If so, the Kor

Memorial Scholarship given by the Klingon Language Institute might provide the cash. Is duck-calling your forte? Well, there's a $1,500 scholarship with your name on it if you win the Chick and Sophie Major Memorial Duck-Calling Contest. *Quack! Quack!*

This Course Is Murder! With 300 students signing up every year, "Murder" is the most popular course ever offered at Amherst College in Massachusetts. Among other things, students read Shakespeare's *Macbeth* and books by Agatha Christie, watch *Pulp Fiction* and *Psycho,* and view *Geraldo* videos. According to Professor Austin Sarat, it's one way to teach students about "great books and moral reasoning."

Whiz Quiz!

At Berlin Technological University, courses are offered in . . .

a. the art of Santahood.
b. how to make a cuckoo clock.
c. the art of strudel making.
d. how to stage an opera.

Take a Vocation:

A Dutch foundation called Facta gives students the chance to meet challenges most of them would never have the opportunity to try. As a result, ten children between the ages of 10 and 17 graduated from flight school in 2004 after only six months of training rather than the standard two years. Besides learning how to fly, the students had to master complicated subjects, such as aerodynamics and meteorology. In the future, Facta hopes to offer courses for kids on investing in stocks and becoming a private detective.

Whiz Quiz!

Wernher von Braun (1912–1977), one of the most famous rocket scientists who ever lived . . .

a. failed math and physics in high school.
b. was home-schooled.
c. skipped three grades in elementary school.
d. did not learn to read until he was seven years old.

What's the big idea? Some ideas are so wacky it's hard to believe that someone didn't just make them up. Three of the statements below are based on actual facts and one is beyond belief. Can you tell which statement is totally bogus?

a. Consultants in New York City are charging $300 an hour to teach parents how to get their children accepted at a good nursery school.

Believe It!   **Not!**

b. To make sure that average students do not feel left out, schools in Nashville, Tennessee, have abolished the honor roll.

Believe It!   **Not!**

c. An environmentally friendly school in Arlington, Virginia, features waterless toilets.

Believe It!   **Not!**

d. To prevent cheating, a school in Wantagh, New York, has students fill out their test sheets in invisible ink.

Believe It!   **Not!**

BONUS QUESTION
Details, Details

Many students find details tedious, but not paying attention to them can sometimes cause a heap of trouble. In 1962, a careless mistake made by a mathematician caused the Atlas Agena B rocket to go off course after takeoff. The spacecraft had to be destroyed—at a loss of $18,500,000! What caused the problem?

a. A misplaced hyphen

b. A multiplication mistake

c. An error in an algebra equation

d. A misplaced decimal point

CHAPTER 3
Nutty Professors

From their extraordinary subject matter to their unusual teaching methods, the instructors you're about to meet probably don't resemble any teachers you've ever had!

It's a Snap:

Coach Mark Davies of Darwin, Australia, has a peculiar method of motivating his 13- to 21-year-old swimmers to break their own records. He drops a crocodile into the pool.

Since Davies started this practice, the swimmers' times have improved considerably.

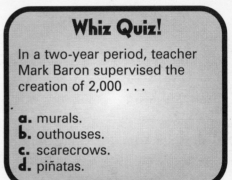

Whiz Quiz!

In a two-year period, teacher Mark Baron supervised the creation of 2,000 . . .

a. murals.
b. outhouses.
c. scarecrows.
d. piñatas.

Class Act:

Dr. George Plitnick, a professor of physics at Frostburg State University in Maryland, dresses up like a wizard to teach a class called "The Science of Harry Potter." With only a few props, such as a petri dish and a bit of liquid nitrogen, Plitnick attempts to answer such questions as: "Can objects really be levitated?" No wonder there's a waiting list to get into this wizard's class!

Class Action: In the late 1970s, high school history teacher Bill Forstchen conducted a simple experiment to show his students firsthand that democracy works best when voters are educated. Calling themselves Young Citizens for Law and Order, the students canvassed Waterville, Maine, with a petition calling for the repeal of laws that favored criminals. Only seven percent of the people approached by the students realized that the laws were actually the Bill of Rights!

Whiz Quiz!

Jonathan Hall, a teacher in Erie, Pennsylvania, teaches physics while . . .

a. leading his students in a jog around the track.
b. lying on a bed of nails.
c. playing his bongo drums.
d. singing the words to music he composed himself.

Elf-ology: Magnus Skarphedinsson of Reykjavik, Iceland, is an elf historian and headmaster of the Icelandic Elf School, which has issued more than 4,000 diplomas in elf studies. According to Skarphedinsson, more than half the population of Iceland believes in elves, dwarfs, gnomes, and other such creatures.

Doggone Amazing: At Dronfield Secondary School in Derbyshire, England, a spaniel by the name of Henry Fanshawe Smart works as a classroom assistant. He was appointed to his position to help teachers deal with student behavioral problems. Henry is so good at his job that as soon as he trots into a room, a group of 30 overly energetic students immediately begin to calm down. Dronfield's grateful human teachers are hoping that Henry will be around for a long time to come!

How Sweet It Is! In 2002, Max Shauck, professor and chair of aviation sciences at Baylor University in Waco, Texas, received the Federal Aviation Administration Excellence in Aviation Award for his research on developing clean, renewable fuels. Shauck is an accomplished pilot, who fuels his own single-engine plane with ethanol—a 180-proof alcohol—which he developed using discarded candy from a local candy factory.

He Speaks Your Language: Willi Melnikov, a professor who lived in Moscow, Russia, could speak 93 different languages!

Whiz Quiz!

Socrates (ca. 470–399 B.C.E.), the famous Greek teacher, was known for his habit of . . .

a. constantly dozing off in class.
b. asking questions about everything.
c. singing patriotic songs every morning.
d. bullying his students.

Long-Distance Teacher:

In the 1980s, retired Air Force Lieutenant Colonel Roger Wells of Valparaiso, Florida, regularly assigned research projects to an English class at a junior high school in New York City, more than 1,000 miles away. Wells broadcast the assignments over shortwave radio and mailed souvenirs  he'd picked up on his world travels to the students who produced the best work.

Stutter-ly Amazing!

John McVicar (1787–1868) cured himself of stuttering by making speeches on the beach  with his mouth full of pebbles. It must have worked because he went on to become a professor of language and speech at Columbia University, where he taught for 47 years!

Red Means Go . . . to the principal's office, that is. In 1982, teachers with lunch duty at Ellendale Elementary School in Memphis, Tennessee, were bothered by the noise level in the students' cafeteria. Their solution? They installed a sound meter and a traffic light. As long as the noise stayed below 72 decibels, the light remained green. If the level went above that number, the light turned yellow—a warning to quiet down. If the noise level didn't go down, the light turned red—the signal for all talking to stop. Anyone still talking when the light was red was sent straight to the principal's office.

Bee-yond Bee-lief: In 1982, an elementary school principal in Colorado got a surprise when he asked his teachers to give him a list of words for a spelling bee. Among the words submitted were "feable" (for feeble), "formorly" (for formerly), and "bookeeping" (for bookkeeping). Good thing the teachers didn't have to participate in the spelling bee!

What's Up, Doc? In 2004, Yuri Shmakov, a teacher in Ulyanovsk, Russia, left his job to start a new career—rabbit breeding. He not only plans to breed rabbits but also to milk them. A single rabbit produces one glass of creamy, high-fat milk a day. It would take 25 rabbits to produce as much milk as one dairy cow, but with the help of a rabbit-sized milking machine, Shmakov hopes to be able to produce enough milk to sell commercially.

Bmal Elttil a Dah Yram: That's not gobbledygook. It's how reading specialist Mary Bakuni of Stamford, Connecticut, reads "Mary had a little lamb." You see, in addition to being a reading teacher, Bakuni has a hidden talent: She can read right to left as easily as she can read left to right. She can write and speak backward as well. Gnitseretni yrev!

Whiz Quiz!

To learn ways to keep their students' minds from wandering, a group of New York City elementary and high school teachers took a special course in . . .

a. tap dancing.
b. circus techniques.
c. animal training.
d. talking trash.

Diamond Jim: When Jim Morris was a science teacher and baseball coach at a high school in Texas, he was great at motivating his kids. One year, Coach Morris promised the players that if they won the district championship, he would try out for a major league baseball team. When the players walked away with the trophy, Morris kept his word. He so impressed the talent scouts for the Tampa Bay Devil Rays with his 98-mile-per-hour fastballs that they signed him on—at the ripe old age of thirty-five! Morris later wrote a book that was made into the 2002 movie called *The Rookie*.

Oops! Teacher John Honey wanted to demonstrate to his students that gambling is a waste of both time and money. Sure that they'd be losers, Honey bought 24 lottery tickets—one for each of his students. Imagine his surprise when one of the tickets turned out to be a winner worth $1,000!

Good Debt:

Ji Ping, the head teacher at an elementary school in Shanghai, China, lets the students borrow grade points against their future marks as long as they agree to pay them back with interest. Ten-year-old Cai Wenyi, who just missed getting the top grade on a math test, was allowed to borrow the point she needed for an A+. That meant that on her next test, two points would be deducted from her final score. Not to worry! Cai got herself out of debt and then some by scoring an extra 19 points on her next exam!

Whiz Quiz!

According to a psychological study, one group of students got better grades than others in their age group because . . .

a. they had no siblings.
b. they came from large families.
c. they kept gerbils as pets.
d. their names were at the beginning of the alphabet, so teachers called on them more frequently.

No Way! In 1979, the school district in Dallas, Texas, was the eighth largest in the country. That same year, teachers took an aptitude test that was meant for 13-year-olds—and more than half the teachers flunked!

Hairy Theory: Aden Alden Gordus, professor of chemistry at the University of Michigan, has made a connection between a person's intelligence and the makeup of his or her hair. After studying hair samples from 800 people, Gordus came to the conclusion that those who had more copper and less iodine, lead, cadmium, and zinc in their hair were the smartest.

No Cheating! In the 1970s, three professors in Puerto Rico were fed up with kids cheating on tests, so they put their heads together to find a way to stop it. The professors came up with a test sheet covered with a type of ink that reflects light, making it impossible for test takers to see the answers of students seated next to them.

Whiz Quiz!

What do schoolteachers get more of than anyone else?

a. Valentines
b. Headaches
c. Apples
d. Free books

Booby Prizes: High school seniors are dying to get into Andrew "Doc" Badger's College Freshman Composition classes at Lecanto High School in Florida, so they can be a part of the legendary awards banquet at the end of the year. Everyone in Doc's class gets a trophy for passing, but the real fun begins when the special awards are passed out. For the best essays in Composition I and II, there are the Pullet-Surprise and the No-Bell Awards. The top prize of the evening is The Golden Caret. Other prizes include a giant Hershey's Kiss for the student who never misses an opportunity to kiss up to the teacher, a Whine-and-Cheese award that goes to the biggest complainer, and a rubber chicken for the student most in love with the sound of his or her own voice.

How Puzzling! Michael Miller was just 15 years old when he became a professor at the New School for Social Research in New York City. His course, "Beyond Crossword Puzzles," helped students develop advanced techniques for figuring out complicated puzzles.

It's the *Principal* of the Thing: Ben Shuldiner, founder of the High School for Public Service in the Crown Heights section of Brooklyn, once played a life-sized Jell-O Pudding Pop on TV. For the nine-year-old child actor, the best part about making the Jell-O commercial was the chance to work with Bill Cosby. Sixteen years later, at the age of 25, Shuldiner became the youngest person in New York State, and maybe in the nation, to become a high school principal. From Pudding Pop to principal—that's pretty impressive!

Whiz Quiz!

In West Virginia, teacher Porter Bennett once taught a class packed with 10 . . .

a. girls and 40 boys.
b. sets of twins.
c. of his own brothers and sisters.
d. of his own children.

Making Headlines! You might think that the following stories were dreamed up by a writer with an overactive imagination. Actually, just one of them was. Can you spot the tall tale?

a. A group of high school teachers at a school in Crawford, Texas, are taking bronco-busting courses to learn how to control rowdy students.

Believe It!   Not!

b. Dr. Hans Gadow (1855–1925), a professor of ornithology (the study of birds) at Cambridge University, tasted several thousand caterpillars to figure out why birds preferred certain types of caterpillars over others.

Believe It!   Not!

c. When teacher Ernest Digweed, of Portsmouth, England, died, he left £26,0000 (about $46,560) to Jesus on the condition that he reappear on Earth no later than the year 2056.

Believe It!   Not!

d. Brian Martin, a physics teacher at a school in St. Catharines, Ontario, Canada, gave his students a final exam in which riding a roller coaster was worth 30 percent of their grade.

Believe It!   Not!

BONUS QUESTION
Clowning Around

During World War II, the British government hired circus clowns to teach soldiers how to . . .

a. make the enemy laugh.

b. amuse themselves in the trenches.

c. fall from planes without injuring themselves.

d. make the enemy think they were so silly they could easily be defeated.

The next time someone starts talking about "the good old days," you can counter with these stories about the past imperfect!

That's Multitasking!

In 1827, teachers in the United States not only had to give lessons but were also required to fill oil lamps, clean out chimneys, and haul coal and water to the schoolhouse.

Whiz Quiz!

Founded in 1635, the first public school in the United States is still operating. Its name is the . . .

a. New York School for Young Scholars.
b. Boston Latin School.
c. Philadelphia Liberty School.
d. Rhode Island School of Classical Studies.

Gotta Dance!

On November 14, 2003, Wheaton College in Wheaton, Illinois, held its first school dance since it was founded in 1860. The reason? Dancing had been prohibited for both teachers and students, whether on- or off-campus, for more than 130 years. In the 1990s, the rules were relaxed to allow students and teachers to dance with relatives at family celebrations. Finally, in 2003, the rules were changed to allow students to dance wherever they like—as long as they do not behave immodestly.

Ouch! In the days of one-room schoolhouses, teachers did not have to spare the rod—literally. Children who misbehaved might be rapped on the knuckles with a ruler, made to wear a dunce cap, ordered to sit in the corner, or told to stand for a period of time with their arms outstretched, sometimes holding a book in one hand.

Golden Rule: The first school in Douglas Flat, California, was built in 1854 during the Gold Rush. Since the building had been constructed on gold-bearing gravel, a part of the teachers' salary was the right to pan for gold during recess.

Whiz Quiz!

A 4,200-year-old tablet was found in a Babylonian school that was excavated in 1894. The tablet bears a proverb that was written by a child, which reads . . .

a. "He who shall excel in a tablet writing shall shine as the sun."
b. "She who rises early shall have the biggest breakfast."
c. "He who befriends a cat will be blessed with good luck."
d. "She who completes her studies will reap multiple rewards."

Isn't It Romantic? In 1880, Robert Greer, a math teacher at the Mount School in York, England, proposed to a woman named Anne with this mathematical formula: If R = 1/2 and A = 1/2, then R + A = 1, but R – A = nothing at all. Her answer? Let it be R + A.

Sandpaper: In the 1700s, schoolchildren of all ages were taught in a single room by the same teacher, and paper was so scarce that students often had to practice their letters on sand-covered boards.

Togetherness: Did you know that there are still some children in the United States who attend one-room schoolhouses? In the early 1900s, there were about 200,000 one-room schoolhouses in the country. By 1997, the number had dropped, but there were still about 450 one-room public schools and more than 700 Amish and Mennonite one-room schools.

Those Kids!

The more things change, the more some things stay the same. Take the generation gap, for instance. The ancient Greek teachers and philosophers were no different from many modern-day teachers who feel they get no respect. Plato's students were just as bad as today's kids. "What is happening to our young people?" he wrote. "They disrespect their elders, and they disobey their parents. They riot in the streets inflamed with wild notions. Their morals are decaying. What is to become of them?" Indeed!

Got It Wrong: Louisa May Alcott (1832–1888), who wrote *Little Women* and is one of America's most beloved authors, once wrote an essay about her experiences as a governess. She sent it to a publisher named James T. Fields, who returned it to her along with a note saying, "Stick to your teaching, Miss Alcott. You can't write."

Whiz Quiz!

For show-and-tell in her kindergarten class, five-year-old Brigitte Berosini, daughter of an animal trainer . . .

a. wore a boa constrictor around her neck.
b. put the family's champion German shepherd through his paces.
c. stuck her head into a lion's mouth.
d. rode on the back of a Siberian tiger.

the just man shall be in eternal remembrance

Went to Prison for Teaching Colored Children.

Boo! Hiss! In January 1832, Connecticut schoolteacher Prudence Crandall (1803–1890) opened an academy for girls. When Crandall admitted Sarah Harris, an African-American, white parents pulled their daughters out of the academy, so Crandall turned it into a school for young African-American women. The state of Connecticut quickly passed the infamous "Black Law," which prohibited the school from operating. Crandall ignored the law and was arrested. She spent only one night in jail but went through three trials before the case was finally dismissed. When a mob attacked the school in September 1834, Crandall was finally forced to close it. Throughout the rest of her life, Crandall taught and spoke out for equality in education and women's rights.

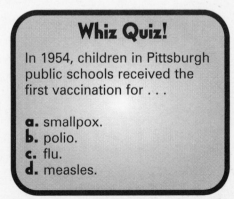

Whiz Quiz!

In 1954, children in Pittsburgh public schools received the first vaccination for . . .

a. smallpox.
b. polio.
c. flu.
d. measles.

Paving the Way: On January 23, 1849, Elizabeth Blackwell (1821–1910) became the first American woman to receive a medical degree. She attended Geneva Medical College (now Hobart and William Smith Colleges) in Geneva, New York, after  the faculty let the students vote on whether or not to admit her. Thinking that admitting a woman was a good joke, the students voted yes. Once in, Blackwell had to fight for the right to attend classes in anatomy—but she still ended up graduating at the top of her class.

All Work, No Play: On March 4, 1842, children got some very good news. A law was passed limiting the hours they were allowed to work. Though children were not required to attend school in those days, they could work for wages. After the law was passed, children under 12 were no longer allowed to work more than ten hours a day. Makes going to school seem like a piece of cake!

Handkerchief, Anyone? Harriet Neild, who taught ancient history at the Mount School in York, England, was such an admirer of the ancient Greeks that during each lecture on the Battle of Thermopylae, she would burst into uncontrollable weeping.

No Way!

Benjamin Franklin (1706–1790), who distinguished himself as one of the finest scientists, inventors, diplomats, and writers in the United States, only attended school from the age of eight to ten!

Whiz Quiz!

Because he suffered from stage fright, Pierre de Montmaur (1564–1648), professor of Greek at the College de Paris, delivered his lectures . . .

a. at the crack of dawn so he always had an empty classroom.

b. wearing a blindfold so he wouldn't have to see his students.

c. after having his students turn their chairs to face the back of the room.

d. with his back to his students.

Nutty Professors

Let's Get Physical: There's a long waiting list of students at Frostburg State University in Maryland, who are dying to get into Dr. George Plitnick's physics course. Could it be because he wears a wizard costume to class?

Elf-ology: Magnus Skarphedinsson of Reykjavik, Iceland, is an elf historian and the headmaster of the Icelandic Elf School, which has issued more than 4,000 diplomas in elf studies.

That's a Croc! Ever since Coach Mark Davies of Darwin, Australia, began tossing a live crocodile into the pool, the kids on his swim team have been moving a whole lot faster!

Special

Balancing Act: Teachers at Alimancani Elementary School in Jacksonville, Florida, see to it that everyone in the school gets to juggle at least once a day. Why? They believe that juggling improves hand-eye coordination, concentration, and confidence—not to mention that it's a lot of fun.

Red Alert: In 2002, the Polish media cited a study that claimed wearing red underwear while taking exams gave students a better chance of passing. Whatever works!

Barking up the Right Tree: Finally, a study kids can be happy about! German psychologist Reinhold Bergler has evidence that children who own dogs make the best students. *Woof! Woof!*

Education

Past Perfect:

To prevent the beautiful Mohawk language from becoming extinct, students at the Mohawk School in Rooseveltown, New York, speak only the native language of their ancestors while in class.

Tsi Iehará·rens

Ónhka?
Ohnihonkiéhrha?
Ka'nón:we?
Kátke?
Ohnonkie·ren?

Math in the Path: At the Gateway School in St. Louis, Missouri, a walkway filled with brightly colored cones is actually a mini lesson in math. Pull the cones apart and you'll have a puzzle of geometric shapes to piece back together.

Teachers' Pets

Purr-fect Attendance: Max the cat followed his owner to school one day, and he's been her classmate ever since. The little guy loves school so much that sometimes he even waits outside the school doors on weekends when no one is there.

Eeek! Imagine reaching for a book on the shelf of the school library and pulling out a snake instead! That's what happened to a student at the Alonsa School in Manitoba, Canada, after the school was plagued by an infestation of garter snakes!

All the Way Home: Because they were rejected by their mother, piglets Wolver and Hampton were being hand-raised by students at the Dean Hall School in New Zealand. When they disappeared from the school grounds on different days, no one thought the newborns could survive on their own. Amazingly, the two very skinny little pigs found each other and returned to the school after 10 days of fending for themselves.

On Guard! When students at the St. Mark's School in Brighton, England, were being dive-bombed on the playground by seagulls, the school hired hawks to come to their rescue.

Paw Power: Capable of controlling a class full of 30 overly-energetic children, this Cavalier King Charles spaniel might be the best classroom assistant the Dronfield Secondary School has ever had!

WAYS TO GO!

Shore to Shore: For many children in Brazil, a boat is the fastest way to get to school.

Getting the Drift: In Alaska, kids don't worry about getting to school in the snow. They just jump on the snowmobile and go!

Fitting In: Children in India pile onto rickshaws to get to school.

Going Underground: Russian schoolchildren wait for the train in a subway station hung with crystal chandeliers.

Above It All: In countries where there are more forests than roads, school buses are out of the question. One way to get to school in the rain forest is to zip above the trees while securely hooked up to a cable.

School Spirits

Seen But Not Heard: On October 3, 1963, a secretary at Nebraska's Wesleyan University walked into an office in the music building and saw a woman in old-fashioned clothes—who then disappeared. Later, the secretary saw a yearbook photo of the woman, a music teacher who had died on October 3, 1936, in that very room.

Yikes! At the Stivers School in Dayton, Ohio, the ghost of a woman with long white hair, who apparently drowned in the school pool in the 1920s, roams the halls. After the school has been locked up for the night, noises can be heard through the windows—by anyone brave enough to stick around, that is!

Boiled Alive! If you were to venture inside the Higginsport School in Ohio, you might hear the cries of a man who burned to death in the boiler room. The school is no longer in use, but it comes to life on Halloween, when people pay to tour the haunted building.

Past imperfect! You probably won't find these school-related facts in your history books, even though three of them are true. Can you spot the one that's totally made up?

a. In Rome, Italy, there's a school for people who want to become gladiators. The students are each given actual Roman names from the time of Emperor Nero (37–68 C.E.) to use while they learn the ancient art of combat.
Believe It!   Not!

b. In Victorian England, the Royal College of Surgeons sold tickets to the public to watch an ancient Egyptian mummy be unwrapped. Even the Archbishop of Canterbury attended.
Believe It!   Not!

c. During the early 1900s, second graders in the Gold Miners School in San Francisco, California, were frightened every third period by the ghost of a child that never failed to moan all through their math lesson.
Believe It!   Not!

d. Mary, the star of the nursery rhyme, was a real little girl who actually did have a little lamb that followed her to school. The girl's name was Mary Sawyer, and she went to a school in Sterling, Massachusetts.
Believe It!   Not!

BONUS GAME
Famous Last Words

Even some of the world's most legendary geniuses were misjudged by their teachers at one time or another. Match the famous person with the less-than-complimentary judgments made about them by their teachers.

1. Author Hans Christian Andersen . . .

2. Composer Guisseppi Verdi . . .

3. Author Emile Zola . . .

4. Mathematical genius Albert Einstein . . .

5. British Prime Minister Winston Churchill . . .

a. was rejected by several music schools.

b. was called careless and forgetful.

c. was told his writing would end up in a trash heap.

d. got zeros in literature and composition.

e. was called a lazy dog by his teacher.

5 Weird and Wacky 101

Here are some bizarre school stories that just might make you appreciate your own school a little more.

Whiz Quiz!

Students at the Massachusetts Institute of Technology once designed a gown that . . .

a. lit up when the person wearing it danced.
b. turned bright orange in the moonlight.
c. radiated heat in cold weather.
d. glowed in the dark.

Blowing His Final:

Matthew Hand, a student at Trent University in Nottingham, England, blew 210 consecutive bubble-gum bubbles as part of his final project in a contemporary art class!

Little Flunkies:

In 1979, a group of parents in Austin, Texas, helped their children study for a kindergarten screening test. The parents coached the children to say, "I don't know," whether they knew the answer or not. That way the kids would be classified as "learning disabled" and allowed to attend a prekindergarten class free of charge. Believe It or Not!

Jammin': Their secret is out. In the winter, kids from a number of schools on Long Island, New York, wear their pajamas inside out. Why? To conjure up a snow day, of course! Sometimes the ritual works, like on the night of January 14, 2004, when enough snow fell to cancel school the next day and it was smooth sledding for all.

Lots of times, though, it doesn't, and kids have to take off their inside-out pajamas, put away their snowsuits, and put on school clothes instead. Bummer!

Boo! In September 2003, 140 students at Goalsara Primary School in West Bengal, India, refused to attend school after a student who went to retrieve a ball that had been kicked into the building came back outside shouting, "Ghosts! Ghosts!" The terrified children took off and, in the confusion, some of them fell and suffered bruises. Naturally, the story grew, and soon everyone was saying that the ghosts had caused the bruises. After two weeks, the teachers finally had to go door-to-door to talk the students into returning to class!

Whiz Quiz!

As an incentive to get them to stop playing hooky, students at Bonnie Doon School in Edmonton, Canada, were offered . . .

a. a free trip to Disney World.
b. a ride in a hot air balloon and a diving lesson.
c. two weeks without any homework.
d. a T-bone steak for lunch every day.

Hey! Carl Grimmer was suspended from his middle school in Richland Hills, Texas, for three days in December 2003 because he sent the greeting "Hey" to every computer in the school. It all started when his dad taught him how to send messages using DOS (Disk Operating System), the operation system that still supports Windows in many PCs. The next day in computer class, the eighth grader showed a friend what he had learned, and off the message went. In no time, the culprit was identified and found guilty of computer tampering. Busted!

Cool Fortune: A high school student in Boynton Beach, Florida, was sitting in a portable classroom in a trailer when he accidentally dropped his pencil into an air conditioning duct. When he tried to fish it out, he found $40,600! Since nobody claimed the money, the student got to keep it!

Whiz Quiz!

A summer program for school children in Powell, Wyoming, offered a cooking class featuring recipes for . . .

a. kangaroo tail soup and seaweed salad.

b. crocodile stew and caramel-covered ants.

c. chocolate-covered grasshoppers and mealworm quiche.

d. fried beetles and bird's nest soup.

Shattering Experience:

As a belated birthday present to his son, British Naval Commander Mark Durkin took the boy to his school in Southsea, England, by helicopter. The treat was spoiled when the winds created by the propellers blew out a plate glass window in the school. Luckily, no one was hurt.

Hiss-terical: For about ten years, the Alonsa School in Manitoba, Canada, was overcrowded every spring and fall—not with students but with hundreds of garter snakes! The snakes were harmless, but listening to them crawl through the ceilings and finding them on library shelves could be pretty creepy. The problem started when an abandoned  basement where the snakes had their den was sealed up, and the snakes moved to the school. To get rid of them, the school had a new, artificial den built.

Sweet Deal: Students at the Falkenberg High School in Sweden are paid the equivalent of $60 a month just to show up at school on time every day!

Hawk Patrol: Seagulls that were building nests on the roof of Barassie Primary School in Ayrshire, England, were terrorizing students by dive-bombing them as they tried to eat their snacks on the playground. To solve the problem, school officials hired two hawk handlers. Now, every morning the handlers release two hawks to scare the seagulls away. Of course, the students are quite grateful, so the handlers give the kids a chance to show their appreciation by allowing them to stroke the impressive birds.

Snow Job: In February 2004, a snowman that had been "kept alive" for more than a year at the Berlin Technical University was allowed to melt. The brainchild of artist and scientist Joerg Jozwiak, the snowman stayed cool in his solar-powered, glass-walled freezer during Germany's record-breaking summer temperatures. Jozwiak was intrigued by the idea of preserving something normally so temporary, while school officials were delighted at the idea of

demonstrating solar power in such an eye-catching way. "We used the snowman's natural enemy—sunshine—to prolong his life," said Jozwiak on the day they pulled the plug on the snowman. "I hereby declare that this very special student . . . is ready to matriculate back into the natural world," he added.

Tough Chicken: The Fightin' Blue Hen is the official mascot of the University of Delaware. Embodied in a giant blue-and-gold bird named YouDee, the mascot may be a chicken, but the athletic teams are not. They have a long tradition of excellence both on the playing field

and in the classroom. The history of the name Fightin' Blue Hens dates back to the Revolutionary War, when a Delaware regiment was said to have battled as ferociously as its distinctive breed of fighting cocks.

Really Bugged: Fordyce High School in Arkansas is the alma mater of the legendary college football coach Paul "Bear" Bryant (1913–1983). The school chose the name Redbugs for its mascot after the day its football players got covered with bug bites during a 1920s game played on an unmown field that was infested with chiggers.

How Cute!

In Omaha, Nebraska, Benson High School is known as the home of the Mighty Bunnies, and in Colorado, a lamb is the mascot of Fort Collins High School, whose students call themselves the Lambkins.

Fighting Artichokes:

Who would choose a vegetable for a mascot? A student body that was staging a protest against the athletic program might. When the Scottsdale Community College administrators shifted funds away from scholarships in order to build a multimillion-dollar football field, many students were outraged. To console them, the administrators told the student body that they could choose the name of the mascot. The students chose the artichoke. Despite the resulting controversy, the school kept the artichoke as a mascot—but have yet to build the football field.

Whiz Quiz!

At the Imperial Primary School of Tokyo, Japan, funeral services were held for . . .

a. the school mascot, a guinea pig.
b. the third grade's goldfish.
c. students' broken dolls.
d. frogs that were dissected in biology class.

Fishing Weather: Imagine gazing out the window of the school bus, when all of a sudden a bunch of fish start pelting the glass. That's exactly what happened in Lincoln County, Maine. A shower of flying fish collided with a school bus driven by George Hutchings. Maybe the fish were hoping to hitch a ride to school!

Fish Story: In February 2004, a fish named Dory saved an elementary school in Eagan, Minnesota, from going up in flames. Responding to a smoke alarm, firefighters arrived at the school to find that the fire was under control. A teacher had forgotten to snuff out a burning candle, which ignited a cardboard box, spread to some workbooks and, finally, to the desk the candle had been sitting on. Before the flames could spread any further, however, the heat from the fire cracked Dory's fish bowl, releasing enough water to dampen the flames. Luckily, there was just enough water left in the bottom of the bowl to keep Dory alive.

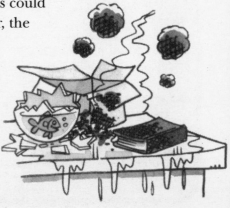

Featherbrained! More than 750 students at Oregon State University took part in a giant pillow fight on campus.

Spin Cycle: A company in the United States has developed a computerized system connected to washers and dryers that can be accessed on the Internet. College students will be able to use their computer to tell whether there are empty machines available and to find out when their clothes are clean or dry! What will they think of next?

Wacky Web Site: Ken Thompson, a British school caretaker, discovered a spiderweb spun by millions of black monkey spiders that covered 11.3 acres of a sports field at Kineton High School.

Shipshape: Blundells' School in Tiverton, England, was built entirely from the wreckage of the Spanish Armada.

Whiz Quiz!

In Florida, it is illegal to . . .

a. chew bubble gum while taking an exam.
b. make faces at a teacher.
c. put livestock on a school bus.
d. take more than two bathroom breaks per class.

The *Hole* Truth! In the Jackson Library at the University of North Carolina there is a 20-year-old doughnut on display. Two decades ago, it was placed on an office radio antenna and instantly improved reception.

Picture This! So you thought learning to write the 26 letters of the English alphabet was hard. Try learning 1,000. That's how many characters or word-pictures, called *kanji,* Japanese children must learn before they graduate from elementary school!

No More Paddle Whacks: In 1980, there was a break-in at the Meadowview Middle School in Morristown, Tennessee. Ten items were stolen—all of them paddles that had been used to punish unruly students.

Whiz Quiz!

The punishment called solitary confinement at Islip Terrace Junior High School on Long Island, New York, requires misbehaving students to . . .

a. spend all day in an empty classroom.
b. spend three hours after school in the principal's office.
c. eat lunch alone.
d. do homework in a glass isolation booth.

Brain Buster

To believe or not to believe—Shakespeare couldn't have said it better! Come to think of it, he did! Only one of these goofy facts is not true. Can you find it?

a. Students at New York City's Cooper Union School once conducted a study to see if there was any way to drop an egg 41 feet without breaking it. One successful egg dropper was Ersy Schwartz, who had tied his egg to an open umbrella!

Believe It!   **Not!**

b. The Wilder Brain Collection at Cornell University in Ithaca, New York, has 650 jars filled with brain specimens, including the brain of its founder, Burt Wilder, who started the collection in the 1980s.

Believe It!   **Not!**

c. To pass Professor Frank French's field biology course at Georgia Southern University, students must first prepare and eat a dish made with weeds and insects.

Believe It!   **Not!**

d. On the first day of school, a fourth grader at Tulsa Elementary School in Oklahoma flew his own helicopter to school.

Believe It!   **Not!**

BONUS QUESTION

What did Dr. William Buckland, the first professor of geology at England's Oxford University, eat at a dinner party?

a. Gold-encrusted partridges that had been marinated in expensive perfume

b. The heart of France's King Louis XIV

c. An omelet sprinkled with ground-up diamonds and pearls

d. The liver of a miner whose perfectly preserved body was found in a peat bog

POP QUIZ

Time to earn some extra credit! Prove how much you remember about wacky students, goofy courses, nutty professors, and those good old-fashioned school days by answering the following questions. The more you get right, the more points you'll rack up on your Ripley's scorecard!

1. Yawning is . . .
a. a sign of disrespect.
b. means your feet are cold.
c. contagious.
d. more common among boys than girls.

2. In 1939, a popular college fad that swept the country was all about . . .
a. cramming as many people as possible into a Volkswagen.
b. wearing beanies backward.
c. swallowing goldfish.
d. wearing saddle shoes.

3. A study done at Colgate University in New York found that people were better at solving math problems when they were lying down with their feet propped up.
Believe It!   **Not!**

4. Scientists think the reason young children learn more quickly than adults is because kids . . .

a. are more curious.

b. are smarter.

c. are less afraid to make mistakes.

d. have more nerve connections in their brains.

5. Some teachers have their students juggle each day because it . . .

a. is a great way to earn a living.

b. helps students do well in school.

c. gives teachers time to read the paper while their students are juggling.

d. helps kids get into college.

6. Children at the Akwesasne Freedom School in Rooseveltown, New York, speak their native language in class because they . . .

a. don't want to speak English.

b. don't know how to speak English.

c. can learn the Mohawk language more easily than English.

d. don't want the Mohawk language to die out.

7. Coach Mark Davies motivates his students to swim faster by . . .

a. throwing a firecracker into the pool.

b. throwing a crocodile into the pool.

c. filling the pool with ice cubes.

d. taking students who break their own records for ice cream after practice.

8. When teachers at the Ellendale Elementary School in Memphis, Tennessee, got tired of the noise level in the cafeteria, they . . .

a. covered the mouths of offenders with duct tape.

b. used a megaphone to shout above the noise.

c. installed a sound meter and traffic light.

d. ate their lunches outside.

9. Dr. George Plitnick's class, called "The Science of Harry Potter," is really a course in . . .

a. physics.

b. biology.

c. geology.

d. wizardry.

10. Louisa May Alcott, who worked as a teacher while writing *Little Women*, was once told by a publisher . . .

a. to change her title to *Little Girls*.

b. that books about women were boring.

c. that women should not write books.

d. to stick to teaching because she was no good at writing.

11. In 1842, a law was passed that made it illegal for children to make fun of their teachers.

Believe It!   **Not!**

12. In 2003, the rules were changed at Wheaton College in Illinois to allow students to . . .

a. stay out past 10:00 P.M. on weeknights.

b. use the library on Sundays.

c. hold picnics on the campus lawn.

d. dance on campus.

13. For a period of about ten years, the Alonsa School in Manitoba, Canada, was infested with . . .

a. fleas.

b. snakes.

c. cockroaches.

d. rats.

14. Students at the Falkenberg High School in Sweden are paid the equivalent of $60 a month for showing up on time each day.

Believe It!   Not!

15. At Berlin Technical School, a snowman was preserved for an entire year . . .

a. in a basement freezer in the Hall of Science.

b. encased in a refrigerated phone booth in the registrar's office.

c. in a solar-powered see-through freezer on the campus lawn.

d. in a glass case kept at the bottom of the deep, icy waters of Lake Bierwurst.

Answer Key

Chapter 1
Odd-inary Students
Page 5:   **c.** Japan.
Page 7:   **c.** did not attend college.
Page 8:   **a.** one free pizza a week for a year.
Page 11:   **a.** balance their schoolbooks on their heads.
Page 12:   **a.** 35 miles long.
Page 15:   **d** red handkerchiefs.
Page 17:   **d.** didaskaleinophobia.
Page 18:   **a.** "foolishly wise."
Page 20:   **d.** Australia.
Brain Buster: b. is false.
Bonus Game: 1.d., 2.f., 3.a., 4.c., 5.b., 6.e.

Chapter 2
A Little Off Course
Page 23:   **c.** rats make happy chirping noises
             when tickled.
Page 25:   **b.** "Comic Book Studies."
Page 26:   **d.** encourage cows to produce more milk.
Page 29:   **d.** TV talk-show host Oprah Winfrey.
Page 31:   **a.** the art of Santahood.
Page 32:   **a.** failed math and physics in high school.
Brain Buster: d. is false.
Bonus Question: a. A misplaced hyphen

Chapter 3
Nutty Professors
Page 35: **c.** scarecrows.

Page 36: **b.** lying on a bed of nails.

Page 38: **b.** asking questions about everything.

Page 41: **b.** circus techniques.

Page 43: **d.** their names were at the beginning of the alphabet, so teachers called on them more frequently.

Page 44: **a.** Valentines

Page 46: **c.** of his own brothers and sisters.

Brain Buster: a. is false.

Bonus Question: c. fall from planes without injuring themselves.

Chapter 4
It's History!
Page 49: **b.** Boston Latin School.

Page 51: **a.** "He who shall excel in tablet writing shall shine as the sun."

Page 53: **d.** rode on the back of a Siberian tiger.

Page 54: **b.** polio.

Page 56: **a.** at the crack of dawn so he always had an empty classroom.

Brain Buster: c. is false.

Bonus Game: 1.c., 2.a., 3.d., 4.e., 5.b.

Chapter 5
Weird and Wacky 101

Page 59: **a.** lit up when the person wearing it danced.

Page 61: **b.** a ride in a hot air balloon and a diving lesson.

Page 62: **c.** chocolate-covered grasshoppers and mealworm quiche.

Page 65: **d.** may be disturbed by the high-frequency noise made by snowflakes melting in the ocean.

Page 67: **c.** students' broken dolls.

Page 69: **b.** attend an opera performance.

Page 70: **c.** put livestock on a school bus.

Page 72: **d.** do homework in a glass isolation booth.

Brain Buster: d. is false.

Bonus Question: b. The heart of France's King Louis XIV

Pop Quiz

1. **c.**
2. **c.**
3. **Believe It!**
4. **d.**
5. **b.**
6. **d.**
7. **b.**
8. **c.**
9. **a.**
10. **d.**
11. **Not!**
12. **d.**
13. **b.**
14. **Believe It!**
15. **c.**

What's Your Ripley's Rank?

Ripley's Scorecard

Congrats! You've busted your brain over some really nutty school facts and proven your ability to tell truth from fiction. Now it's time to rate your yourself. Are you **Barely Passing** or will you get **Top Marks**? Check out the answers in the Answer Key and use this page to keep track of how many trivia questions you've answered correctly. Then add them up and find out how you rate.

Here's the scoring breakdown—give yourself:
★ **10 points** for every **Whiz Quiz!** you answered correctly
★ **20 points** for every fiction you spotted in the Ripley's Brain Busters
★ **10 points** for every **Bonus Game** or **Question** solved
★ and **5 points** for every Pop Quiz question you answered correctly.

Here's a tally sheet:
Number of **Whiz Quiz!**
questions answered correctly: _____ x 10 = _____
Number of **Ripley's Brain Buster**
fictions spotted: _____ x 20 = _____
Number of **Bonus Games** or
Questions you solved: _____ x 10 = _____
Number of **Pop Quiz** questions
answered correctly: _____ x 5 = _____

Final score: _____

0–100
Barely Passing!

Maybe you haven't been paying enough attention or maybe you're just not that motivated to read about school—after school! No problem. There are plenty of Ripley's books about other subjects. Do you love animals? Pick up *Awesome Animals* to find out some startling facts about our furry friends. Or if you're into extremes, try *X-traordinary X-tremes* to find out about everything from extreme sports to extreme creations.

101–250
Extra Credit!

Give yourself an A for effort! It's obvious that you're starting to develop a taste for weird and wacky school stories. When it comes to separating fact from fiction, you've definitely got a line on the amazing world of Robert Ripley! Keep it up, and it won't be long before you're collecting your own tales of the unbelievable!

251–400
Gold Star!

There's no doubt about it. You're a fast learner and you've got a knack for telling the unbelievable but true from the unbelievable and totally untrue! You may not have passed every Whiz Quiz! but with just a little more practice, you'll soon be getting Top Marks on the Ripley's scorecard!

401–575
Top Marks!

Congratulations! You're at the head of the class when it comes to bizarre and unbelievable facts! Clearly, the usual is too ho-hum for you! Who needs to read about boring everyday subjects when you can spend your hours wandering the halls of Ripley's school of the strange and unusual? Still, it might be wise to spend some of your time studying. You never know when you're going to have to pass a pop quiz that really counts!

Believe It!®

Photo Credits

Ripley Entertainment Inc. and the editors of this book wish to thank the following photographers, agents, and other individuals for permission to use and reprint the following photographs in this book. Any photographs included in this book that are not acknowledged below are property of the Ripley Archives. Great effort has been made to obtain permission from the owners of all materials included in this book. Any errors that may have been made are unintentional and will gladly be corrected in future printings if notice is sent to Ripley Entertainment Inc., 7576 Kingspointe Parkway, Suite 188, Orlando, Florida 32819.

Black-and-White Photos

6   David Letterman/Kevin Winter/DMI/ Time Life Pictures/Getty Images

10 Teenager/BananaStock/BananaStock, Ltd./PictureQuest

13 Teenage Girl Studying; 65 Snowman/ © Creatas/PictureQuest

15 Robert F. Kennedy/Hulton Archive/Getty Images

16 Fourth-Grade Students/Courtesy of Veterans Memorial Elementary School

19 Greg Smith/International Youth Advocates

25 Gateway School/EDAW, Inc.

26 Students Juggling/Courtesy of Dave Finnigan/www.icanjuggle.com

28 Endeavor Elementary School Students/ © Dan Lamont

31 Klingons/Everett Collection, Inc.

36 Dr. George Plitnick/Associated Press

37 Henry Fanshawe Smart/The Dronfield School

41 Rabbit/Photodisc Green/Getty Images

42 Jim Morris/Doug Pensinger/Getty Images

45 Lecanto High School Student/Courtesy of Andrew "Doc" Badger

46 Ben Shuldiner/Ari Mintz/Copyright, 2004, Newsday. Reprinted with permission.

50 Dancers; 62 Computer Monitor/Ablestock

52 One-room Schoolhouse; 54 Prudence Crandall/Library of Congress

60 Kids in Pajamas/Kathy Kmonicek/ Copyright, 2004, Newsday. Reprinted with permission.

66 YoUDee/Courtesy of the University of Delaware

71 Brush/© Royalty-free/CORBIS

Color Insert

(1) Dr. George Plitnick/Associated Press; Elf/Getty Images; Crocodile/Creatas/ Creatas/PictureQuest; Background/Photodisc Green/Getty Images

(2-3) Students Juggling/Courtesy of Dave Finnigan/www.icanjuggle.com; Student and Dog/Lucidio Studio Inc./CORBIS; Mohawk Student/Melanie Weiner; Gateway School, Background/EDAW, Inc.

(4-5) Girl with Cat, Background/The Image Bank/Getty Images; Library, Seagulls/ Photodisc Red; Garter Snake/Gary M. Stolz/U.S. Fish and Wildlife Service; Piglets/Hulton Archive/Getty Images; Henry Fanshawe Smart/The Dronfield School

(6-7) Students in Canoe/Victor Englebert; Snowmobile/© Karen Robinson/Panos Pictures; Students in Rickshaw/© Mark Henley/Panos Pictures; Russian Subway, Background/Stone/Getty Images; Zip Line/ Ben Fraser

(8) Teacher/Nebraska Wesleyan University; Stivers School, Higginsport School/Robert Hock/www.rhock.com; Background/Taxi/ Getty Images

Cover

Main Image: Dog with Mortarboard/Taxi/ Getty Images; Circles: Girl Blowing Bubble, Teacher/© Corbis Images/PictureQuest; Pig/Digital Vision

Don't miss these  other exciting **Believe It or Not!** books . . .

World's Weirdest Critters

Creepy Stuff

Odd-inary People

Amazing Escapes

World's Weirdest Gadgets

Bizarre Bugs

Blasts from the Past

Awesome Animals

Weird Science

X-traordinary X-tremes

WE'D LOVE TO BELIEVE
YOU!

Do you have a Believe It or Not!
story that has happened to you or to someone
you know? If it's weird enough and if you would
like to share it, the people at Ripley's would love
to hear about it. You can send your
Believe It or Not! entries to:

**The Director of the Archives
Ripley Entertainment Inc.
7576 Kingspointe Parkway,
Suite 188
Orlando, Florida 32819**

Believe It!®